Alpha Male

Master the Art of Influence, Dominate Your Domain, and Achieve Success in Every Area of Life

Lewis Finan

Table of Contents

Introduction

In the grand tapestry of human existence, there exists a timeless archetype—the Alpha Male. Enigmatic, charismatic, and commanding, the Alpha Male is a symbol of unwavering confidence, magnetic influence, and unparalleled success. From the realms of business to personal relationships, the Alpha Male navigates life with a purposeful stride, leaving an indelible mark on every sphere of existence.

Welcome to "Alpha Male: Master the Art of Influence, Dominate Your Domain, and Achieve Success in Every Area of Life." This book is not just a manual; it's a roadmap for those who aspire to embody the essence of the Alpha Male—a figure that transcends mere dominance and steps into the realm of genuine leadership.

In these pages, we will delve into the psyche of the Alpha Male, unraveling the layers that define his mindset, behavior, and ultimately, his success. Whether you are a seasoned entrepreneur, a budding professional, or an individual seeking personal growth, the principles within these chapters will empower you to harness the Alpha within.

The journey begins with an exploration of the traits that distinguish the Alpha Male. Confidence, resilience, and a strategic mindset are the cornerstones upon which the Alpha builds his empire. Through real-world examples, psychological insights, and practical exercises, we will guide you in cultivating these qualities within yourself.

But an Alpha is not merely an island unto himself. The art of influence, a skill mastered by the Alpha, is a central theme throughout this book. You will discover how to navigate social dynamics, inspire others, and build a network that propels you towards your goals. Unleash the power of charisma, communication, and emotional intelligence to become a force that shapes the world around you.

As we delve into the professional domain, you will learn how the Alpha Male approaches challenges, makes decisions, and cultivates a mindset of relentless achievement. From boardrooms to entrepreneurial ventures, the principles outlined here will empower you to lead with conviction and excel in the competitive landscapes of your chosen field.

Yet, the Alpha's influence extends beyond the office walls. Relationships, whether personal or romantic, are a crucial facet of a fulfilled life. In the latter sections of this book, we explore how the Alpha Male navigates the intricate dance of human connections, fostering meaningful relationships and leaving a lasting impact on those he encounters.

"Alpha Male" is not about conforming to stereotypes or promoting an antiquated view of masculinity. Instead, it's a call to embrace the qualities that define true leadership, regardless of gender. It's about cultivating strength, wisdom, and authenticity to become the master of your destiny.

Are you ready to embark on a transformative journey? Prepare to unlock your potential, command respect, and achieve unparalleled success. The path of the Alpha Male awaits, and this book is your guide. Let the transformation begin.

Unveiling the Alpha Male Concept

In the intricate dance of human behavior and societal dynamics, the concept of the Alpha Male stands as a powerful and often misunderstood archetype. Far more than a mere label associated with dominance or bravado, the Alpha Male embodies a set of traits and principles that transcend stereotypes and conventional thinking. In this exploration, we peel back the layers of the Alpha Male concept to reveal a nuanced understanding that goes beyond simplistic notions of dominance.

At its core, the Alpha Male concept is rooted in the idea of leadership—a leadership not defined by force, but by a unique combination of confidence, resilience, and strategic thinking. Unlike the outdated image of a chest-thumping, overbearing figure, the true Alpha Male is a master of self-assurance, possessing an unwavering belief in his abilities and a calm assertiveness that commands respect.

Confidence, a hallmark of the Alpha Male, is not a superficial facade but a deep-seated understanding of one's worth and capabilities. It is the quiet assurance that emanates from knowing oneself and embracing strengths and weaknesses alike. Through this lens, the Alpha Male navigates challenges with grace, recognizing setbacks as opportunities for growth rather than deterrents.

Resilience, another key facet of the Alpha Male concept, underscores the ability to weather storms and emerge stronger on the other side. Life is a series of challenges, and the Alpha Male approaches adversity not with defeatism but with an indomitable spirit. Every setback becomes a stepping stone, and every failure a lesson that propels him forward.

Strategic thinking forms the backbone of the Alpha Male's approach to life. Far from impulsive or reactionary, the Alpha Male plans strategizes, and executes precisely. This strategic mindset extends beyond personal endeavors to encompass leadership in various spheres—in the boardroom, within a team, or even within the dynamics of personal relationships.

It's crucial to dispel the notion that the Alpha Male concept is confined to gender stereotypes. While historically associated with masculinity, the traits encapsulated in the Alpha Male concept—confidence, resilience, strategic thinking, and leadership—are not exclusive to any gender. Women, too, can embody these qualities, forging their paths with strength and purpose.

As we delve deeper into the Alpha Male concept, we will explore the dynamics of influence—the art through which an Alpha Male leaves a lasting impact on those around him. From effective communication to cultivating charisma and emotional intelligence, the Alpha Male's influence extends far beyond the superficial realms of dominance.

Join us on this exploration as we demystify the Alpha Male concept, recognizing its universal applicability and embracing the principles that foster genuine leadership. This journey is not about conforming to stereotypes but about unlocking the potential within each individual to become a guiding force in their own lives and the lives of others. The Alpha Male concept is a call to authenticity, strength, and the relentless pursuit of excellence. Let the unveiling begin.

The Power of Influence

In the intricate web of human interactions, influence emerges as a formidable force that shapes decisions, drives change, and leaves an indelible mark on the tapestry of relationships and societies. Understanding the nuances of influence is akin to unlocking a potent source of power—one that, when wielded with wisdom and integrity, can propel individuals to new heights of success and transform the very fabric of the world around them.

At its essence, influence is not a mere transactional exchange but a complex interplay of communication, charisma, and the subtle art of persuasion. It is the ability to inspire, guide, and effect change in others by tapping into a deep understanding of human psychology and social dynamics.

The influential individual possesses a keen awareness of the impact of words and actions. Communication, the bedrock of influence, transcends the mere transmission of information; it becomes a vessel for inspiration, motivation, and connection. The power to articulate thoughts with clarity and resonance enables an individual to transcend boundaries, fostering a shared understanding that forms the basis of influence.

Charisma, often regarded as an elusive quality, is a magnetic force that draws people toward the influencer. It emanates from authenticity, confidence, and a genuine passion for the subject at hand. Charismatic individuals possess an innate ability to captivate audiences, leaving a lasting impression that lingers in the minds of those they encounter.

Emotional intelligence, a crucial component of effective influence, involves the ability to empathize, understand, and connect with others on a profound level. By discerning the emotions and motivations that drive human behavior, influencers can tailor their messages to resonate with the core values and aspirations of their audience, creating a resonance that transcends the superficial.

The power of influence extends beyond individual interactions to permeate the spheres of leadership, entrepreneurship, and social change. Leaders who master the art of influence inspire loyalty, galvanize teams, and steer organizations toward success. Entrepreneurs who understand the dynamics of consumer influence wield the ability to shape markets and innovate with impact. Advocates for social change leverage influence to rally communities, challenge norms, and pave the way for a better future.

However, the true power of influence is not solely measured by the scale of one's impact but by the ethical foundation upon which it rests. Influencers who wield their power responsibly recognize the weight of their words and actions, using their influence to uplift, empower, and contribute positively to the collective well-being.

In the pages that follow, we will delve into the strategies, principles, and ethical considerations that define the power of influence. Whether you aspire to lead, inspire, or effect change, the insights within will guide you on a transformative journey, unlocking the potential to become a force for good in a world shaped by the art of influence. Join us as we explore the dynamic landscape of influence and harness its power to create meaningful, lasting impact.

Chapter 1: Understanding Alpha Traits

In the pursuit of mastering the Alpha Male persona, the foundation lies in a comprehensive understanding of the key traits that define this archetype. The Alpha Male is not a one-dimensional figure; rather, he is a dynamic amalgamation of qualities that set him apart in the realms of confidence, resilience, and strategic thinking. In this chapter, we embark on a journey of exploration, dissecting the core attributes that form the bedrock of the Alpha Male's identity.

1. Confidence: The Cornerstone of Alpha Presence

Confidence is the pillar upon which the Alpha Male stands tall. It is not the brash arrogance often misconstrued, but a deep-rooted belief in one's abilities and inherent worth. We delve into the psychology of genuine confidence, exploring how self-assurance shapes actions, decisions, and the overall demeanor of the Alpha Male.

2. Resilience: Navigating Challenges with Grace

Life is a series of challenges, and the Alpha Male approaches adversity not as a roadblock but as a stepping stone to growth. Resilience, a defining trait, is examined in its various dimensions. From bouncing back after setbacks to maintaining composure under pressure, we unravel the resilience that propels the Alpha Male forward in the face of obstacles.

3. Strategic Thinking: The Mindset of a Master Planner

The Alpha Male is not a creature of impulse but a strategic thinker who plans and executes with precision. This section dissects the strategic mindset that distinguishes the Alpha Male in both personal and professional spheres. We explore how strategic thinking influences decision-making, goal-setting, and the navigation of complex challenges.

4. Authentic Leadership: Guiding with Purpose

Leadership, within the context of the Alpha Male, transcends traditional notions. It is about authenticity, leading by example, and inspiring others to reach their full potential. This section examines the principles of authentic leadership that set the Alpha Male apart as a guide and mentor in various aspects of life.

5. Gender Neutrality: Embracing Alpha Traits for All

While historically associated with masculinity, the traits encapsulated in the Alpha Male concept are not exclusive to any gender. In this subsection, we discuss how both men and women can embody these traits, fostering a broader understanding of the Alpha Male archetype that goes beyond gender stereotypes.

As we unpack these fundamental Alpha traits, the goal is not to conform to a rigid mold but to empower individuals to cultivate these qualities authentically. Through practical insights, real-world examples, and actionable exercises, this chapter serves as a roadmap for readers to begin their journey toward understanding and embodying the traits that define the Alpha Male. Whether you are an aspiring leader, entrepreneur, or someone seeking personal growth, the lessons within will lay the groundwork for a transformative evolution. Join us as we delve into the multifaceted world of Alpha traits and pave the way for a journey of self-discovery and empowerment.

1.1 Confidence: The Core of Alpha Presence

In the intricate tapestry of the Alpha Male persona, confidence emerges as the keystone, the unwavering foundation upon which the entire presence is built. Beyond the superficial veneer of arrogance, true confidence is an internal force—a deep, unshakable belief in one's capabilities and inherent worth. In this section, we embark on a profound exploration of confidence, unraveling its nuances and understanding how it forms the beating heart of Alpha's presence.

1. Genuine Confidence Unveiled

Genuine confidence is not a façade; it's a state of being. We delve into the psychology of authentic confidence, exploring how self-assurance emanates from a thorough understanding of one's strengths, competencies, and potential. It is the quiet certainty that transcends external validations, grounding the Alpha Male in a steadfast belief in himself.

2. The Body Language of Confidence

Confidence is not merely verbal; it's a language communicated through posture, gestures, and expressions. We dissect the body language of the Alpha Male, unveiling the subtle cues that convey assurance and dominance. From a purposeful stride to the magnetic power of eye contact, we explore how non-verbal communication becomes a canvas for projecting confidence.

3. Embracing Vulnerability as Strength

Paradoxically, the Alpha Male's confidence is not threatened by vulnerability; it is strengthened by it. We discuss the concept of confident vulnerability—the ability to acknowledge imperfections and learn from failures without compromising self-esteem. Understanding how vulnerability and confidence coexist is a key aspect of cultivating a resilient and genuine Alpha presence.

4. Confidence in Decision-Making

Confidence is palpable in the decisions an Alpha Male makes. Whether navigating professional challenges or personal choices, the ability to make decisions with conviction stems from a confidence rooted in self-trust. We explore the link between confidence and effective decision-making, emphasizing the importance of trusting one's instincts.

5. Cultivating Confidence Authentically

Confidence is not a mask one puts on; it's a quality that grows from within. This section provides practical insights and exercises to help readers cultivate confidence authentically. From positive self-talk to embracing challenges as opportunities, these strategies pave the way for a genuine and enduring sense of confidence.

As we navigate the terrain of confidence, it is essential to recognize that the Alpha Male's assurance is not about overshadowing others or projecting false bravado. Instead, it is a beacon that inspires, uplifts, and invites others to walk alongside. Join us on this journey into the core of Alpha presence, where confidence reigns supreme, and discover how unlocking this internal force can reshape your path to success and fulfillment.

1.2 Leadership Instincts

Leadership, at its core, is an intricate dance between strategic decision-making, emotional intelligence, and the instinctual ability to guide others toward a common goal. In this exploration of "Leadership Instincts," we unravel the innate qualities that set exceptional leaders apart—the instincts that go beyond learned skills and emerge from a deep understanding of oneself, the team, and the dynamic environment in which leadership unfolds.

1. Visionary Intuition

Leadership often begins with a vision—an intuitive foresight that transcends the immediate challenges. We delve into the concept of visionary intuition, exploring how exceptional leaders possess an innate ability to anticipate trends, foresee opportunities, and envision a compelling future. This instinctual foresight becomes the North Star that guides decision-making and inspires collective action.

2. Empathetic Connection

At the heart of effective leadership lies the ability to connect with others on a profound level. Empathetic instincts enable leaders to understand the diverse perspectives, needs, and aspirations of their team members. We explore how empathetic leadership fosters a culture of trust, collaboration, and mutual respect, creating a cohesive environment where everyone feels heard and valued.

3. Adaptive Resilience

Leadership is not a linear journey; it's a dynamic expedition filled with unexpected twists and turns. Exceptional leaders exhibit adaptive resilience—an instinctual response to challenges that combines flexibility, perseverance, and a willingness to learn. We examine how leaders navigate uncertainties, pivot in the face of adversity, and lead their teams with unwavering resolve.

4. Decisive Instincts

The ability to make timely and effective decisions is a hallmark of strong leadership. Decisive instincts involve synthesizing information swiftly, trusting one's judgment, and taking calculated risks. We explore how leaders balance the need for thorough analysis with the imperative to act decisively, understanding that indecision can be a greater risk than imperfect decisions.

5. Inspiring Influence

Influence is not coerced but earned through authentic leadership. Leaders with inspiring instincts have the power to motivate and mobilize others toward a shared purpose. We delve into the art of influential leadership, examining how charismatic communication, a compelling narrative, and a genuine passion for the mission create a magnetic pull that transcends traditional authority.

6. Servant Leadership

An often overlooked yet powerful instinct is the inclination toward servant leadership. Exceptional leaders understand that their role is to serve the greater good of the team and the organization. We explore how leaders with a servant's heart inspire loyalty, foster a culture of collaboration, and elevate the collective success of the entire group.

7. Continuous Learning Reflex

Leadership is a journey of perpetual growth. The instinct to embrace continuous learning is a distinguishing feature of effective leaders. We discuss how leaders cultivate a learning reflex—remaining curious, seeking feedback, and adapting their leadership style based on evolving circumstances.

As we navigate the landscape of leadership instincts, it becomes evident that exceptional leaders are not bound by a rigid set of rules but guided by an intuitive understanding of themselves and the ever-changing dynamics of leadership. Whether you are a seasoned executive, an emerging leader, or someone aspiring to lead in various facets of life, the insights within this exploration will illuminate the path to becoming a leader who instinctively inspires, guides, and shapes a better future.

1.3 Assertiveness in Action

Assertiveness, often misconstrued as mere outspokenness, is a nuanced and indispensable trait that empowers individuals to express their needs, opinions, and boundaries while respecting those of others. In this exploration of "Assertiveness in Action," we delve into the dynamic interplay of self-assurance, effective communication, and the art of setting boundaries to foster healthy relationships and achieve personal and professional success.

1. Understanding Assertiveness

At its core, assertiveness is the confident and respectful expression of one's thoughts, feelings, and needs. We unravel the distinctions between assertiveness, passivity, and aggression, providing a foundation for understanding the assertive mindset and its transformative impact on interactions.

2. The Power of Clear Communication

Assertiveness thrives on clear and articulate communication. We delve into the language of assertiveness—how to convey ideas with clarity, use "I" statements to express feelings, and actively listen to others. From workplace scenarios to personal relationships, effective communication becomes the linchpin for asserting oneself without diminishing others.

3. Setting and Communicating Boundaries

Healthy relationships are built on clear boundaries. We explore the assertive art of setting and communicating boundaries, understanding that this is not an act of exclusion but a vital step toward self-respect and mutual understanding. From professional collaborations to personal dynamics, the ability to articulate and uphold boundaries is central to assertive living.

4. Navigating Conflict with Confidence

Conflict is an inevitable aspect of life, and assertiveness provides a constructive framework for navigating it. We discuss how assertive individuals approach conflict with confidence, addressing issues directly, seeking compromise, and maintaining composure. The assertive response to conflict is a powerful tool for fostering understanding and resolution.

5. Saying "No" with Grace

The assertive ability to say "no" is liberating, not confrontational. We explore the art of declining requests or obligations without guilt or undue explanation. Saying "no" with grace is an essential skill that preserves personal boundaries, maintains focus, and cultivates a balanced and fulfilling life.

6. Building Self-Confidence

Assertiveness and self-confidence are intertwined. We delve into strategies for building and bolstering self-confidence, recognizing that a strong sense of self-worth forms the bedrock of assertive behavior. From positive affirmations to celebrating achievements, we explore practices that empower individuals to assert themselves with authenticity.

7. Cultural Sensitivity in Assertiveness

Assertiveness takes on different shades in diverse cultural contexts. We examine how cultural sensitivity enhances assertiveness, acknowledging that effective communication requires an understanding of cultural nuances. By navigating these subtleties, assertive individuals bridge gaps, foster inclusivity, and build meaningful connections across cultural boundaries.

As we embark on the journey of assertiveness in action, the goal is not dominance but empowerment—empowerment to express oneself authentically, engage in constructive dialogue, and cultivate relationships built on mutual respect. Whether you're navigating professional challenges, seeking to enhance personal relationships, or aiming for self-improvement, the principles and practices within this exploration will guide you toward mastering assertiveness in your actions, interactions, and the pursuit of a more assertive and fulfilling life.

Chapter 2: Mastering the Art of Influence

In the intricate dance of human interactions, the ability to wield influence emerges as a powerful force that shapes destinies, fosters collaboration and drives positive change. "Mastering the Art of Influence" is a journey into the realms of persuasion, charisma, and authentic connection—an exploration of the skills and principles that elevate individuals to become true masters of influence.

1. The Psychology of Persuasion

At the heart of influence lies the psychology of persuasion. We delve into the cognitive and emotional factors that underpin effective persuasion, examining how understanding the minds of others becomes a cornerstone for influencing decisions and behaviors.

2. Charismatic Communication

Charisma is a magnetic quality that draws people in and inspires them to follow. This section explores the elements of charismatic communication, from the power of storytelling to the nuances of body language. Uncover the secrets of charismatic leaders and learn how to infuse your communication with authenticity and allure.

3. Emotional Intelligence in Influence

Emotional intelligence forms the bedrock of influential connections. We dissect the role of empathy, self-awareness, and social skills in navigating the complex landscape of human emotions. Discover how emotional intelligence enhances your ability to relate to others, building trust and strengthening the bonds of influence.

4. Adapting Influence Styles

Influence is not a one-size-fits-all endeavor. We explore various influence styles—analytical, assertive, and inspiring—and discuss how adapting your approach to different situations and personalities maximizes your impact. Whether leading a team or negotiating a deal, understanding the versatility of influence styles becomes a strategic advantage.

5. Building a Persuasive Narrative

The art of influence often hinges on the ability to craft a compelling narrative. Learn the elements of storytelling that captivate and persuade, whether in a boardroom presentation, a sales pitch, or a casual conversation. A persuasive narrative weaves facts with emotion, creating a tapestry that resonates with your audience.

6. The Influence of Ethical Leadership

True influence transcends personal gain; it serves a higher purpose. We delve into the concept of ethical leadership and how leading with integrity amplifies the impact of influence. Explore the long-term benefits of ethical influence in fostering trust, loyalty, and sustainable success.

7. Navigating Resistance and Overcoming Objections

Influence encounters resistance, but adept influencers see challenges as opportunities. This section explores strategies for navigating resistance, handling objections, and turning skepticism into collaboration. By understanding the sources of resistance, you gain the tools to overcome obstacles on the path to influence.

As we venture into the realm of mastering the art of influence, remember that true influence is a harmonious blend of authenticity, empathy, and strategic communication. Whether you aspire to lead teams, build meaningful relationships, or effect positive change, the insights and skills within this chapter will empower you to navigate the complexities of influence and emerge as a masterful influencer in every facet of your life. Join us as we unravel the secrets, hone our skills, and embark on the transformative journey of mastering the art of influence.

2.1 Persuasion Techniques for Alpha Males

In the pursuit of mastering the art of influence, Alpha Males harness a set of persuasive techniques that align with their confident and assertive demeanor. These techniques, rooted in charisma, strategic thinking, and effective communication, enable Alpha Males to navigate diverse scenarios with finesse. In this exploration, we unveil persuasion strategies tailored to complement the Alpha Male persona.

1. Confident Body Language

Technique: Power Pose

Alpha Males understand the significance of non-verbal communication. Adopting a power pose—standing tall, shoulders back, and exuding confidence—sends a strong visual message. This technique not only conveys assurance but also influences the perception of those around, establishing a foundation for persuasive interactions.

2. Strategic Framing

Technique: Positioning as a Solution Provider

Alpha Males strategically frame their ideas as solutions to challenges. By showcasing how their proposals address specific needs or concerns, they position themselves as problem solvers. This framing taps into the innate leadership instincts of Alpha Males, making their perspectives compelling and persuasive.

3. Charismatic Storytelling

Technique: Narrative Appeal

Alpha Males leverage the power of storytelling to captivate their audience. Through vivid and engaging narratives, they create an emotional connection. This technique not only makes their messages memorable but also fosters a sense of camaraderie, enhancing the persuasive impact of their communication.

4. Active Listening and Adaptation

Technique: Empathetic Engagement

While Alpha Males are known for their assertiveness, they equally recognize the importance of active listening. By genuinely understanding the perspectives of others, Alpha Males adapt their communication style. This empathetic engagement builds rapport, establishing a foundation for effective persuasion.

5. Confident Verbal Communication

Technique: Clear and Concise Expression

Alpha Males excel in clear and concise verbal communication. They articulate their ideas with precision, avoiding unnecessary details. This technique not only projects confidence but also ensures that their messages are easily digestible, enhancing the likelihood of acceptance.

6. Social Proof Utilization

Technique: Highlighting Successes

Alpha Males subtly incorporate social proof into their persuasive arsenal by highlighting past successes. Whether personal achievements or team victories, showcasing a track record of success reinforces their credibility. This technique establishes them as credible leaders worth following.

7. Strategic Use of Authority

Technique: Confident Command

Alpha Males recognize the influence of authority. When delivering a persuasive message, they do so with a confident command that reflects their leadership status. This technique aligns with their natural inclination to lead, making their recommendations more compelling.

8. Creating a Sense of Urgency

Technique: Strategic Timeliness

Alpha Males infuse a sense of urgency into their persuasive efforts. Whether in decision-making or rallying a team, they emphasize the timely nature of their proposals. This technique taps into the Alpha Male's proactive mindset, encouraging swift and decisive action.

In mastering persuasion techniques, Alpha Males navigate the fine line between assertiveness and collaboration. By blending their innate confidence with these strategic approaches, they create a persuasive presence that leaves a lasting impact in both professional and personal spheres. These techniques serve not only as tools for influence but also as expressions of the authentic Alpha Male persona.

2.2 Building a Network of Power

In the dynamic landscapes of professional and personal success, the ability to cultivate a network of power is a strategic advantage that transcends traditional networking. Building meaningful connections, influencing decision-makers, and fostering collaborative alliances form the core of a powerful network. In this exploration, we unveil the principles and strategies for constructing a network of power that propels individuals toward their goals.

1. Strategic Relationship Building

Approach: Quality over Quantity

A powerful network is not defined by the sheer number of connections but by the depth and strategic relevance of relationships. Alpha Males prioritizes cultivating meaningful connections with individuals who bring value, insights, and opportunities. Quality relationships form the bedrock of a network of power.

2. Effective Communication Skills

Skill: Charismatic Expression

Alpha Males understand the impact of charismatic communication. The ability to articulate ideas with clarity, confidence, and charisma enhances the influence within the network. Whether conveying a vision or negotiating a deal, effective communication skills set the stage for building and leveraging power.

3. Strategic Networking Events

Tactic: Selectivity in Attendance

Rather than attending every networking event, Alpha Males strategically choose gatherings aligned with their goals. Whether industry conferences or exclusive forums, these events provide targeted opportunities to connect with influential individuals, amplifying the effectiveness of their networking efforts.

4. Leveraging Existing Relationships

Strategy: Mutual Value Creation

Alpha Males recognize the symbiotic nature of powerful networks. By actively seeking ways to contribute to the success of others within their network, they foster a culture of mutual value creation. This approach solidifies existing relationships and opens doors to new possibilities.

5. Online Presence and Branding

Tool: Strategic Digital Presence

In the digital era, an online presence is a powerful tool for network building. Alpha Males strategically curates their digital footprint, using platforms such as LinkedIn to showcase expertise, share insights, and connect with influential professionals. This digital branding extends the reach and impact of their network.

6. Confidence in Networking

Mindset: Confident Engagement

Alpha Males approach networking with a confident mindset. They view interactions not as mere exchanges but as opportunities to showcase their strengths and make a lasting impression. Confidence in networking establishes a magnetic presence that attracts influential connections.

7. Strategic Mentorship and Advisory Relationships

Approach: Seeking Guidance and providing it

Alpha Males actively seek mentorship from individuals with valuable experience. Simultaneously, they offer mentorship to those seeking guidance. This two-way approach strengthens their network by creating a web of mutually beneficial relationships and fostering a culture of collective growth.

8. Navigating Power Dynamics

Skill: Strategic Awareness

Understanding power dynamics within a network is crucial. Alpha Males navigates these dynamics with strategic awareness, recognizing the influencers, decision-makers, and thought leaders. This awareness guides their interactions, allowing them to position themselves strategically within the network hierarchy.

9. Follow-up and Relationship Maintenance

Practice: Consistent Engagement

Building a network of power is an ongoing process. Alpha Males prioritize consistent follow-up and engagement. Whether through periodic check-ins, sharing relevant resources, or acknowledging achievements, they actively maintain and nurture relationships within their network.

In the realm of power networking, Alpha Males combine their natural confidence with strategic approaches, creating a network that amplifies their influence and opens doors to new opportunities. This intentional and value-driven network building is not just about personal success; it's about creating a web of influence that benefits all connected. Through these principles and strategies, individuals can forge a network of power that propels them toward unprecedented heights of success and impact.

2.3 Charisma and Its Impact

Charisma, that intangible quality that captivates and inspires, is a magnetic force shaping perceptions, influencing decisions, and leaving a lasting imprint on human interactions. In this exploration, we delve into the essence of charisma, examining its components, unraveling its impact, and understanding how individuals can harness this powerful quality to elevate their personal and professional endeavors.

1.   The Essence of Charisma

Charisma is more than mere charm; it's an alchemy of traits and behaviors that draw people in. Confidence, authenticity, and the ability to connect emotionally form the core of charismatic individuals. Understanding the essence of charisma involves embracing these qualities and projecting them with sincerity.

2.   The Power of Presence

At the heart of charisma lies a compelling presence that commands attention. Charismatic individuals exude a magnetic energy that captivates those around them. Whether in a boardroom, on a stage, or in a one-on-one conversation, the power of their presence leaves a lasting impression.

3. Authenticity as a Charismatic Force

Authenticity is the bedrock of charisma. Charismatic individuals are genuine and true to themselves, creating a sense of trust and relatability. The impact of authenticity resonates deeply, fostering connections that extend beyond surface interactions.

4. Emotional Resonance

Charisma is not solely about words; it's about evoking emotions. Charismatic individuals have a unique ability to connect with the emotions of others, creating a shared experience. This emotional resonance forms a bridge that strengthens relationships and influences perceptions.

5. Confident Communication

Charismatic communication is marked by confidence and clarity. Whether articulating ideas, delivering a presentation, or engaging in casual conversation, charismatic individuals speak with conviction. The impact of confident communication extends to inspiring others and instilling confidence in their abilities.

6. Adaptability and Relatability

Charisma is not a one-size-fits-all quality. Charismatic individuals possess an adaptability that allows them to connect with diverse audiences. This relatability is a dynamic aspect of charisma, enabling individuals to resonate with people from different backgrounds and perspectives.

7.   Inspiration and Motivation

Charismatic leaders have the power to inspire and motivate others to action. Through their words, actions, and vision, they instill a sense of purpose and enthusiasm. The impact of this inspiration ripples through teams, organizations, and communities, driving positive change.

8.   The Ripple Effect of Charisma

The impact of charisma extends far beyond individual interactions. Charismatic individuals create a ripple effect, influencing the energy of a room, the dynamics of a team, and the culture of an organization. This ripple effect amplifies their influence and shapes the collective experience.

9.   Charisma as a Leadership Asset

In leadership, charisma is a potent asset. Charismatic leaders inspire loyalty, foster engagement, and navigate challenges with grace. The impact of charismatic leadership is evident in the cohesive and motivated teams they cultivate, contributing to organizational success.

10. Cultivating Charisma

Charisma is not solely an inherent trait; it can be cultivated. Charismatic individuals engage in self-reflection, hone their communication skills, and actively work on building authentic connections. Cultivating charisma involves an ongoing commitment to personal growth and a genuine desire to connect with others.

In the tapestry of human interactions, charisma emerges as a transformative force. Its impact is felt in the connections forged, the inspiration imparted, and the positive influence wielded. By understanding the essence of charisma and actively cultivating its components, individuals can unlock the potential to leave a lasting, positive impact in every sphere of their lives.

Chapter 3: Dominating Your Domain

In the pursuit of success and personal mastery, the concept of "Dominating Your Domain" stands as a beacon for individuals striving to leave an indelible mark in their chosen arenas. This chapter is a journey into the mindset, strategies, and principles that empower individuals—Alpha Males and aspirants alike—to assert their influence, achieve excellence, and carve out a position of dominance in their respective domains.

1. The Dominant Mindset

Mindset Shift: From Competing to Dominating

Dominating your domain begins with a mindset shift. It's not about competing with others; it's about transcending competition and dominating through excellence. This section explores the mental framework that empowers individuals to set their sights on unparalleled achievement.

2. Strategic Excellence

Approach: Strategies for Unrivaled Performance

Dominance is rooted in strategic excellence. Whether in business, sports, or personal pursuits, this section delves into the strategies that set the stage for unrivaled performance. From goal setting to meticulous planning, individuals learn to navigate the path from competence to dominance.

3. Leadership Mastery

Skill Development: Becoming the Dominant Leader

Dominating your domain requires leadership mastery. This section dissects the qualities that define dominant leaders—vision, decisiveness, and the ability to inspire. Individuals learn to step into leadership roles with confidence, driving their teams and organizations toward unparalleled success.

4. Innovative Disruption

Tactic: Championing Change and Innovation

Dominance often emerges from disruptive innovation. Individuals are guided through the art of challenging the status quo, fostering a culture of innovation, and strategically disrupting existing norms to position themselves at the forefront of their domains.

5. Adaptability and Resilience

Trait Development: Thriving in Dynamic Environments

Dominating a domain requires adaptability and resilience. This section explores how individuals can cultivate these traits, navigating challenges and setbacks with a determination that not only ensures survival but propels them forward toward dominance.

6. Strategic Networking for Dominance

Approach: Building Alliances for Collective Dominance

Dominating your domain is not a solitary endeavor. Strategic networking becomes a key component. Individuals learn to cultivate alliances, leverage networks, and create collaborative ecosystems that amplify their impact and contribute to collective dominance.

7. Brand Building and Reputation Management

Practice: Crafting a Dominant Persona

In the era of personal branding, individuals are guided through the process of building a dominant persona. From cultivating a strong online presence to managing reputational capital, this section empowers individuals to craft an image that resonates with dominance in their chosen domain.

8. Continuous Improvement and Mastery

Commitment: The Journey of Lifelong Dominance

Dominance is not a destination but a continuous journey of improvement and mastery. This section instills the commitment to lifelong learning, refinement of skills, and the pursuit of excellence that ensures individuals remain at the forefront of their evolving domains.

9. Ethical Dominance

Principle: Dominance Rooted in Integrity

True dominance is sustainable only when rooted in ethical principles. Individuals are guided through the importance of ethical conduct, transparency, and responsible leadership in establishing and maintaining dominance with integrity.

As individuals delve into the principles and strategies outlined in this chapter, they embark on a transformative journey toward dominating their respective domains. Whether in business, leadership, or personal pursuits, the insights within this exploration serve as a roadmap for individuals seeking not only success but a sustained and influential dominance in their chosen fields. Join us as we unravel the keys to mastering your domain and emerging as a dominant force in the realms of achievement and influence.

3.1 Strategies for Professional Success

Achieving professional success is a multi-faceted journey that requires a combination of skills, mindset, and strategic approaches. This chapter explores a comprehensive set of strategies designed to guide individuals on the path to success in their professional endeavors.

1.   Clarify Your Goals and Vision

Action Step: Define Your Professional Aspirations

Professional success begins with a clear vision of your goals. Take the time to articulate your long-term objectives, both personal and career-related. This clarity becomes the guiding force that shapes your decisions, actions, and professional trajectory.

2.   Invest in Continuous Learning

Practice: Embrace Lifelong Learning

In the rapidly evolving professional landscape, staying relevant is key. Commit to continuous learning by acquiring new skills, staying informed about industry trends, and seeking opportunities for professional development. This proactive approach ensures that you remain adaptable and ahead of the curve.

3. Cultivate a Strong Work Ethic

Trait Development: Demonstrate Diligence and Commitment

A strong work ethic is the foundation of professional success. Demonstrate diligence, reliability, and commitment to your work. Consistently delivering high-quality results not only builds your reputation but also positions you as a valuable and trusted contributor.

4. Build and Leverage Your Network

Approach: Strategic Relationship Building

Networking is a powerful tool for professional success. Cultivate relationships with colleagues, mentors, and industry peers. Actively participate in networking events, engage in online professional communities, and leverage these connections for mutual growth and opportunities.

5. Master Effective Communication

Skill Development: Refine Your Communication Skills

Effective communication is a cornerstone of professional success. Hone your verbal and written communication skills, ensuring clarity, conciseness, and professionalism. The ability to convey ideas, collaborate with others, and articulate your value is critical in any professional setting.

6.   Embrace Adaptability

Mindset Shift: Thriving in Change

In dynamic work environments, adaptability is a distinguishing trait. Cultivate a mindset that embraces change and uncertainty. Demonstrate flexibility in your approach, and view challenges as opportunities for growth. Adaptability ensures you remain resilient and responsive to evolving circumstances.

7.   Strategic Time Management

Practice: Prioritize and Organize Effectively

Effective time management is a skill that directly impacts productivity and success. Prioritize tasks based on importance and deadlines, organize your schedule efficiently, and avoid multitasking when possible. Strategic time management allows you to focus on high-impact activities.

8.   Seek and Provide Constructive Feedback

Behavioral Practice: Foster a Culture of Feedback

Both seeking and providing constructive feedback are crucial for professional growth. Actively seek feedback on your performance and use it as a tool for improvement. Simultaneously, offer constructive feedback to colleagues, fostering a culture of continuous improvement within your professional sphere.

9. Showcase Leadership Qualities

Trait Development: Lead by Example

Leadership qualities go beyond formal titles. Demonstrate initiative, take on leadership responsibilities when appropriate, and lead by example. Proactively contribute to team success, inspire others through your actions, and showcase qualities that distinguish you as a leader.

10. Navigate Challenges with Resilience

Mindset Resilience: Bounce Back from Setbacks

Resilience is the ability to navigate challenges and setbacks with grace. Develop resilience by reframing setbacks as opportunities for learning, maintaining a positive mindset, and leveraging adversity to fuel personal and professional growth.

By integrating these strategies into your professional journey, you embark on a path that not only leads to success but also fosters a fulfilling and impactful career. Each strategy contributes to a holistic approach, empowering you to navigate the complexities of the professional landscape with confidence and purpose.

3.2 Navigating Corporate Environments

Navigating the intricate landscape of corporate environments requires a blend of strategic thinking, interpersonal skills, and a keen understanding of organizational dynamics. This section provides insights and strategies for individuals seeking to thrive and excel within the complex structures of corporate settings.

1. Understanding Organizational Culture

Insight: Decode Values and Norms

Corporate success is often intertwined with organizational culture. Take the time to understand the values, norms, and expectations that define the culture of your workplace. This understanding serves as a compass, guiding your actions and decisions within the corporate context.

2. Strategic Relationship Building

Approach: Forge Genuine Connections

Building strong relationships is pivotal in corporate environments. Forge genuine connections with colleagues, superiors, and cross-functional teams. Cultivate a network that extends beyond immediate job responsibilities, as these relationships can be instrumental in career advancement and navigating organizational challenges.

3.   Effective Communication in the Corporate Arena

Skill Development: Navigate Hierarchies with Clarity

Communication in corporate settings requires finesse. Tailor your communication style to navigate hierarchical structures, ensuring clarity and professionalism. Whether communicating with peers, supervisors, or subordinates, articulate your ideas with precision and adapt your messaging to suit different audiences.

4.   Strategic Self-Advocacy

Practice: Articulate Your Value

Effectively navigating corporate environments involves strategic self-advocacy. Clearly articulate your skills, accomplishments, and contributions. Ensure that decision-makers are aware of your impact, positioning yourself as a valuable asset to the organization.

5.   Mastering Office Politics

Insight: Navigate with Diplomacy

Office politics is an inherent aspect of corporate life. Master the art of navigating office politics with diplomacy and tact. Avoid unnecessary conflicts, build alliances judiciously, and focus on collaborative efforts that contribute positively to team dynamics.

6.   Continuous Learning and Skill Development

Commitment: Stay Relevant in a Dynamic Landscape

Corporate environments are dynamic, with evolving skill requirements. Demonstrate a commitment to continuous learning and skill development. Stay informed about industry trends, attend relevant training programs, and proactively acquire the skills that align with the evolving needs of your role.

7.   Strategic Time and Priority Management

Practice: Balance Demands Effectively

Corporate settings often entail multiple responsibilities and competing priorities. Develop strong time management skills to balance tasks efficiently. Prioritize effectively, delegate when necessary, and ensure that you allocate time to high-impact activities that align with organizational goals.

8. Navigating Performance Reviews and Advancement Opportunities

Approach: Proactively Manage Your Career

Take a proactive approach to managing your career within the corporate structure. Prepare for performance reviews by documenting your achievements and setting future goals. Seek feedback and guidance from mentors or supervisors, and actively explore advancement opportunities aligned with your career objectives.

9. Emotional Intelligence in Corporate Interactions

Trait Development: Navigate Emotions Effectively

Emotional intelligence is a valuable asset in corporate interactions. Develop the ability to understand and manage your emotions, as well as empathize with the emotions of others. This skill enhances your interpersonal effectiveness and contributes to a positive and collaborative corporate culture.

10. Strategic Planning for Long-Term Success

Mindset Shift: Align Actions with Long-Term Goals

Navigate corporate environments with a long-term perspective. Align your actions and decisions with your career goals. This strategic approach ensures that each step contributes to your overall professional growth and success within the organization.

By incorporating these insights and strategies into your approach, you can navigate corporate environments with resilience, strategic acumen, and a focus on sustained success. Successfully maneuvering within the complexities of corporate life requires a combination of interpersonal skills, self-awareness, and a commitment to ongoing growth and development.

3.3 Entrepreneurial Alpha Mindset

The entrepreneurial alpha mindset is a dynamic and assertive approach to business and leadership, characterized by confidence, resilience, and a strategic vision. Embracing this mindset positions individuals as proactive creators, risk-takers, and innovators within the entrepreneurial landscape. Here are key principles and characteristics that define the entrepreneurial alpha mindset:

1. **Visionary Leadership**

Trait: Forward-Thinking Vision

The entrepreneurial alpha mindset is anchored in visionary leadership. Alphas in the entrepreneurial realm possess a clear and compelling vision for their ventures. They anticipate market trends, envision future possibilities, and inspire their teams with a shared purpose.

2. Fearless Risk-Taking

Characteristic: Courageous Pursuit of Opportunities

Entrepreneurial alphas are not averse to risk; they see it as an inherent part of the entrepreneurial journey. They courageously pursue opportunities, understanding that calculated risks can lead to innovation, growth, and the realization of their ambitious goals.

3. Resilience in the Face of Challenges

Trait: Bounce-Back Resilience

Challenges and setbacks are inevitable in entrepreneurship. The entrepreneurial alpha mindset is marked by resilience—the ability to bounce back from failures, learn from setbacks and adapt strategies in the face of adversity.

4. Proactive Problem Solving

Approach: Strategic Solution-Oriented Thinking

Entrepreneurial alphas approach challenges with a proactive and solution-oriented mindset. Rather than dwelling on problems, they focus on identifying strategic solutions. This approach not only resolves immediate issues but also fosters a culture of innovation and continuous improvement.

5. Confidence and Self-Belief

Characteristic: Unwavering Self-Confidence

Confidence is a cornerstone of the entrepreneurial alpha mindset. Alphas believe in their abilities and the value they bring to the table. This self-confidence enables them to make bold decisions, navigate uncertainties, and inspire confidence in their teams and stakeholders.

6. Agile Adaptability

Trait: Flexible and Agile Decision-Making

In the dynamic landscape of entrepreneurship, adaptability is crucial. Entrepreneurial alphas embrace change and exhibit agile decision-making. They pivot when necessary, capitalize on emerging opportunities, and navigate evolving market conditions with strategic flexibility.

7. Innovative Thinking

Characteristic: Constant Pursuit of Innovation

The entrepreneurial alpha mindset thrives on innovative thinking. Alphas are perpetual innovators, constantly seeking new ideas, processes, and products. They foster a culture of creativity within their teams, driving innovation as a key driver of entrepreneurial success.

8.   Ownership and Accountability

Approach: Taking Full Responsibility

Entrepreneurial alphas take ownership of their ventures and actions. They accept accountability for outcomes, whether positive or negative. This sense of responsibility fosters a culture of accountability within their organizations, driving a commitment to excellence.

9.   Strategic Networking and Alliances

Practice: Building Strategic Collaborations

Recognizing the importance of networks, entrepreneurial alphas actively engage in strategic networking. They build alliances with other entrepreneurs, industry leaders, and key influencers. These collaborations contribute to shared learning, market expansion, and a broader impact.

10. Continuous Learning and Adaptation

Commitment: Lifelong Learning and Evolution

The entrepreneurial alpha mindset embraces a commitment to continuous learning. Alphas understands that the business landscape evolves, and staying at the forefront requires ongoing education, exploration of emerging trends, and a commitment to personal and professional development.

Embracing the entrepreneurial alpha mindset is not only about achieving individual success but also about creating a lasting impact in the entrepreneurial ecosystem. By embodying these principles, individuals can navigate the complexities of entrepreneurship with confidence, innovation, and a relentless pursuit of excellence.

Chapter 4: Achieving Success in Relationships

Success in relationships transcends the personal realm, extending its influence into every facet of life, from professional collaborations to personal connections. This chapter delves into the intricacies of cultivating and sustaining successful relationships, offering insights and strategies that empower individuals to build meaningful connections, foster understanding, and navigate the complexities of human interaction.

1. The Foundation of Authentic Connection

Principle: Building Genuine Bonds

Successful relationships are rooted in authenticity. This section explores the importance of genuine self-expression, active listening, and mutual understanding as the foundational elements of authentic connections. Learn to cultivate relationships that go beyond surface interactions, fostering a sense of trust and authenticity.

2. Effective Communication Dynamics

Skill Development: Mastering the Art of Communication

Communication is the lifeblood of successful relationships. Uncover the nuances of effective communication—expressing thoughts clearly, utilizing non-verbal cues, and navigating conflicts with empathy.

Enhance your ability to convey emotions, thoughts, and intentions in a way that strengthens rather than hinders relationships.

3. Empathy and Emotional Intelligence

Trait Development: Understanding and Relating to Others

Empathy is the bridge that connects individuals in meaningful relationships. Explore the role of emotional intelligence in understanding and relating to the emotions of others. Cultivate empathy as a core trait that deepens connections and creates a supportive environment for success in various relationships.

4. Building Trust and Reliability

Approach: Fostering Trustworthy Connections

Trust forms the bedrock of successful relationships. Delve into the principles of trust-building, including consistency, reliability, and transparent communication. Understand how trustworthy behavior contributes to the longevity and depth of relationships in both personal and professional spheres.

5. Navigating Conflict Constructively

Skill Development: Turning Challenges into Growth Opportunities

Conflict is an inevitable aspect of relationships, but its resolution is pivotal for success. Learn constructive strategies for navigating conflicts, turning challenges into opportunities for growth and understanding. Discover the art of compromise, active listening, and fostering resolutions that strengthen rather than strain relationships.

6. Cultivating Positive Relationship Habits

Practice: Nurturing Long-Term Success

Successful relationships thrive on positive habits. Explore practices that nurture and sustain long-term success, from expressing gratitude to actively celebrating achievements. Develop a set of habits that contribute to the overall health and vitality of your relationships.

7. Balancing Independence and Interdependence

Mindset Shift: Fostering Healthy Autonomy

Achieving success in relationships involves finding the delicate balance between independence and interdependence. Understand the importance of maintaining individual identities while fostering a sense of shared goals and mutual support. Embrace a mindset that values both autonomy and interconnectedness.

8. Cultural Sensitivity in Relationships

Insight: Navigating Diverse Perspectives

In our interconnected world, cultural sensitivity is essential for successful relationships. Explore how an awareness of diverse cultural perspectives enhances communication, fosters inclusivity, and creates a foundation for meaningful connections. Learn to navigate cultural nuances with respect and openness.

9. Personal Growth within Relationships

Commitment: Evolving Together

Successful relationships contribute to personal growth and development. Commit to evolving together with your partners, friends, and colleagues. Explore how shared aspirations, mutual support, and a commitment to continuous improvement contribute to the success and fulfillment of everyone involved.

10. Fostering Success in Professional Relationships

Application: Applying Relationship Skills in the Workplace

Extend the principles of successful relationships to the professional arena. Understand how effective communication, trust-building, and conflict resolution contribute to success in team dynamics, leadership, and collaborative endeavors. Apply relationship skills to foster a positive and productive work environment.

As you embark on the journey of achieving success in relationships, recognize that these principles are interconnected, forming a holistic approach to meaningful connections. Whether in personal or professional realms, the insights and strategies within this chapter serve as a guide to cultivate relationships that not only endure but thrive, contributing to a life rich in fulfillment and shared success.

4.1 Alpha Male Dynamics in Personal Connections

The concept of the alpha male extends beyond traditional notions of leadership and influence; it permeates personal connections, shaping dynamics in friendships, romantic relationships, and familial bonds. In this exploration, we delve into the alpha male dynamics within personal connections, examining the traits, behaviors, and strategies that contribute to impactful and fulfilling relationships.

1.   Confidence as a Magnet for Connection

Trait: Attracting through Self-Assurance

In personal connections, the alpha male exudes confidence as a magnetic force. Confidence not only draws others in but also sets the tone for positive interactions. By projecting assurance in oneself and one's choices, the alpha male establishes a foundation for authentic and influential personal connections.

2.   Assertiveness in Setting Boundaries

Behavior: Clear Boundaries, Respectful Engagement

The alpha male navigates personal connections with assertiveness, setting clear boundaries while engaging with respect. This balance ensures that relationships are founded on mutual understanding, where each individual's needs and limits are acknowledged and honored.

3.   Leadership in Nurturing Relationships

Approach: Taking the Lead in Relationship Growth

In personal connections, the alpha male exhibits leadership in nurturing and fostering relationship growth. Whether in friendships or romantic partnerships, the alpha male takes an active role in guiding the relationship forward, steering it toward shared goals and experiences.

4.   Empathy and Understanding

Trait Development: Navigating Emotions with Sensitivity

Contrary to stereotypes, the alpha male is not devoid of empathy. Successful personal connections require an understanding of others' emotions. The alpha male balances strength with sensitivity, demonstrating empathy and a capacity to comprehend the feelings and perspectives of those around them.

5. Effective Communication in Intimate Bonds

Skill Development: Expressing Clearly and Listening Actively

Alpha males excel in effective communication within personal connections. They articulate their thoughts with clarity and actively listen to the concerns of others. This skill fosters open dialogue, contributing to deeper understanding and intimacy in friendships and romantic relationships.

6. Initiative in Relationship Activities

Behavior: Taking Charge in Shared Experiences

In personal connections, the alpha male takes initiative in planning and engaging in shared activities. This proactive approach injects vitality into relationships, ensuring that experiences are purposeful and contribute to the overall growth and enjoyment of the connection.

7. Championing Mutual Growth

Mindset: Fostering Personal and Collective Development

The alpha male mindset extends to championing not only personal growth but also the growth of those in their personal circle. Whether through encouragement, shared goals, or constructive feedback, the alpha male fosters an environment where everyone can strive for continuous improvement.

8. Resilience in Overcoming Challenges

Trait: Navigating Setbacks with Strength

Personal connections inevitably face challenges. The alpha male brings resilience to the table, navigating setbacks with strength and determination. This resilience contributes to the enduring quality of relationships, demonstrating a commitment to overcoming obstacles together.

9. Demonstrating Vulnerability

Approach: Balancing Strength with Authentic Vulnerability

While strength is a hallmark, the alpha male understands the power of vulnerability in personal connections. By sharing genuine emotions and allowing for vulnerability, the alpha male creates a space for authentic and deep connections, fostering intimacy and trust.

10. Balancing Independence and Interdependence

Mindset Shift: Cultivating Autonomy within Connection

In personal connections, the alpha male strikes a balance between independence and interdependence. Recognizing the importance of individual identities, the alpha male cultivates autonomy while fostering a strong and supportive network of personal connections.

Navigating personal connections with alpha male dynamics is a nuanced and multifaceted endeavor. By embracing these principles, individuals can contribute to the creation of robust, meaningful, and enduring personal connections, characterized by authenticity, mutual growth, and a shared journey toward success and fulfillment.

4.2 Balancing Power and Compassion

The delicate interplay between power and compassion forms the foundation for effective leadership, impactful relationships, and a harmonious society. Striking the right balance between these two forces requires thoughtful consideration, self-awareness, and a commitment to values that honor both strength and empathy.

1. Empowering Leadership

Balance: Inspiring Through Empowerment

Leaders who balance power and compassion understand that true empowerment lies in lifting others up. They use their influence to inspire, guide, and enable those around them. By empowering others to reach their full potential, these leaders cultivate a culture of shared success.

2. Transparent Communication

Approach: Clarity and Emotional Connection

Balancing power and compassion in communication involves transparency and emotional connection. Leaders and individuals alike strive to articulate their thoughts with clarity while acknowledging the emotional impact of their words. This approach fosters understanding and a sense of shared purpose.

3. Fair Decision-Making

Trait Development: Equity and Consideration

Balancing power and compassion in decision-making requires a commitment to fairness and consideration. Leaders weigh the impact of their choices on individuals and the broader community, ensuring that decisions align with values of justice, equality, and empathy.

4. Cultivating Emotional Intelligence

Skill Development: Understanding and Navigating Emotions

Individuals who balance power and compassion prioritize emotional intelligence. This skill involves understanding and navigating emotions—both one's own and others'. By fostering emotional intelligence, leaders create environments where empathy coexists with the assertiveness needed to drive positive change.

5. Collaborative Problem-Solving

Approach: Harnessing Collective Strengths

Balancing power and compassion is evident in collaborative problem-solving. Instead of imposing solutions, individuals work together, leveraging diverse perspectives and strengths. This collaborative approach not only addresses challenges effectively but also builds a sense of collective ownership.

6. Accountability with Compassion

Mindset Shift: Encouraging Growth through Accountability

Balancing power and compassion involves holding oneself and others accountable with a compassionate mindset. Instead of punitive measures, the emphasis is on growth and learning. This approach fosters a culture where mistakes are opportunities for improvement rather than reasons for blame.

7. Service-Oriented Leadership

Mindset: Leading with a Focus on Service

Leaders who balance power and compassion adopt a service-oriented mindset. They view their role as a service to others, using their power to facilitate positive outcomes and support the well-being of those they lead. This approach creates a culture of mutual support and shared success.

8. Inclusive Decision-Making

Practice: Welcoming Diverse Perspectives

Balancing power and compassion is reflected in inclusive decision-making. Leaders actively seek input from diverse voices, ensuring that decisions reflect a broad range of perspectives. This inclusivity contributes to a sense of belonging and shared ownership within the community or organization.

9. Strength in Vulnerability

Trait Development: Authenticity in Leadership

Leaders who balance power and compassion embrace the strength found in vulnerability. They authentically share their challenges, uncertainties, and aspirations, creating an environment where others feel comfortable doing the same. This openness fosters genuine connections and trust.

10. Generosity of Spirit

Practice: Fostering a Culture of Generosity

Individuals who balance power and compassion embody a generosity of spirit. Whether through mentorship, recognition, or simple acts of kindness, they contribute to a positive and supportive culture. This generosity reinforces the idea that power can be a force for good and compassion a guiding principle.

Striking the right balance between power and compassion is an ongoing journey of self-discovery and intentional practice. Those who successfully navigate this dynamic interplay create environments where strength and empathy coexist, fostering not only individual success but also a collective sense of well-being and fulfillment.

4.3 Communication Mastery

Communication is the bedrock of human connection and the cornerstone of success in various aspects of life. Communication mastery goes beyond the ability to convey information; it encompasses the art of fostering understanding, building meaningful relationships, and influencing positive outcomes. This exploration delves into the key principles and strategies for achieving communication mastery.

1. Clarity in Expression

Skill: Crafting Clear and Concise Messages

Communication mastery begins with clarity. Successful communicators articulate their thoughts in a clear and concise manner. This involves organizing ideas logically, choosing a precise language, and ensuring that the intended message is easily understood by the audience.

2. Active Listening

Trait Development: Engaging with Full Presence

Mastery in communication involves not only speaking effectively but also listening actively. Cultivating the ability to fully engage in conversations, absorb information, and demonstrate genuine interest in others contributes to a richer and more impactful communication dynamic.

3. Empathetic Communication

Approach: Understanding and Validating Emotions

Empathy is a cornerstone of communication mastery. It involves understanding the emotions and perspectives of others and responding in a way that validates their experiences. Empathetic communication fosters connection, trust, and mutual understanding.

4. Adaptability in Style

Skill Development: Tailoring Communication to the Audience

Masters of communication recognize the importance of adaptability. They tailor their communication style to suit the preferences and needs of their audience. This may involve adjusting tone, language, and delivery to resonate effectively with diverse individuals and groups.

5. Non-Verbal Proficiency

Skill: Harnessing the Power of Body Language

Communication extends beyond words. Masters of communication pay attention to non-verbal cues such as body language, facial expressions, and gestures. Understanding and utilizing non-verbal communication enhances the overall effectiveness of the message.

6. Confidence and Presence

Trait Development: Projecting Assurance and Authority

Confidence is a key element of communication mastery. Individuals who communicate with confidence exude authority and assurance. This trait captivates the attention of the audience and instills a sense of credibility in the speaker.

7. Constructive Feedback

Approach: Providing and Receiving Feedback Skillfully

Effective communication includes the ability to deliver and receive constructive feedback. Masters of communication navigate feedback conversations with tact, focusing on growth and improvement rather than criticism. This skill fosters a culture of continuous learning.

8. Storytelling Prowess

Skill: Crafting Compelling Narratives

Storytelling is a powerful tool in communication mastery. The ability to weave compelling narratives captivates listeners, making information more memorable and relatable. Masters of communication leverage storytelling to convey complex ideas and evoke emotional responses.

9. Conflict Resolution Skills

Skill Development: Navigating Disagreements with Diplomacy

Communication mastery extends to conflict resolution. Skilled communicators navigate disagreements with diplomacy, actively listening to opposing views, finding common ground, and fostering solutions that benefit all parties involved.

10. Strategic Persuasion

Approach: Influencing with Ethical Persuasion

Mastery in communication includes the ability to persuade ethically. Strategic persuasion involves presenting ideas convincingly, appealing to emotions and logic, and inspiring action. This skill is particularly valuable in leadership, sales, and various professional contexts.

11. Cultural Sensitivity

Insight: Navigating Cultural Nuances

In a globalized world, communication mastery includes cultural sensitivity. Understanding and respecting cultural nuances in communication enhance cross-cultural interactions and contributes to effective communication in diverse environments.

12. Digital Communication Proficiency

Skill Development: Navigating Virtual Communication

In today's digital age, mastery in communication extends to virtual platforms. Proficiency in email etiquette, video conferencing, and other digital communication tools is essential for effective communication in professional and personal settings.

13. Continuous Improvement Mindset

Commitment: Committing to Lifelong Learning

True communication mastery is a journey, not a destination. Committing to continuous improvement involves seeking feedback, staying informed about evolving communication trends, and adapting one's skills to navigate the dynamic landscape of human interaction.

In mastering communication, individuals unlock the potential to build meaningful relationships, lead with influence, and contribute positively to personal and professional spheres. This journey is a continuous evolution, marked by intentional practice, self-reflection, and a genuine commitment to the art and science of effective communication.

Chapter 5: Physical and Mental Mastery

In the pursuit of holistic well-being and personal excellence, the synergy between physical and mental mastery forms the cornerstone of a fulfilling and purpose-driven life. This chapter explores the interplay between physical health and mental resilience, providing insights and strategies for individuals seeking to optimize both aspects of their well-being.

1.   **The Mind-Body Connection**

Insight: Understanding the Integral Relationship

Physical and mental mastery are intricately connected, each influencing the other in profound ways. This section explores the symbiotic relationship between physical health and mental well-being, emphasizing the importance of a balanced approach to achieve overall mastery.

2.   **Physical Fitness for Mental Clarity**

Practice: Harnessing Exercise for Cognitive Wellness

Physical fitness is not solely about aesthetics; it is a powerful tool for enhancing mental clarity and cognitive function. Explore the impact of regular exercise on mental well-being and learn practical ways to incorporate physical activity into daily life for optimal mental performance.

3. Nutrition as Fuel for the Mind

Approach: Nourishing the Brain for Mental Mastery

The food we consume has a direct impact on cognitive function. Delve into the role of nutrition in mental mastery, understanding how dietary choices can support brain health, enhance focus, and contribute to sustained mental energy and resilience.

4. Mindfulness and Stress Management

Skill Development: Cultivating Mental Resilience

Mental mastery involves the skill of managing stress and fostering mindfulness. Explore techniques for cultivating resilience, navigating stressors, and incorporating mindfulness practices into daily life to promote mental well-being.

5. Quality Sleep for Optimal Performance

Practice: Prioritizing Rest for Mental and Physical Vitality

Sleep is a cornerstone of both physical and mental health. This section delves into the importance of quality sleep, and its impact on cognitive function, emotional well-being, and physical recovery. Learn strategies for optimizing sleep patterns for overall vitality.

6.   Holistic Approaches to Mental Wellness

Approach: Integrating Holistic Practices

Mental wellness encompasses a holistic approach that extends beyond traditional methods. Explore integrative practices such as meditation, mindfulness, and breathwork that contribute to mental clarity, emotional balance, and overall mental resilience.

7.   Cognitive Enhancement Strategies

Skill Development: Sharpening Mental Acuity

Mental mastery involves strategies for cognitive enhancement. From brain-training exercises to continual learning, this section provides insights into maintaining and improving cognitive function throughout various stages of life.

8.   Balancing Physical Goals with Mental Health

Mindset Shift: Harmonizing Ambition and Well-Being

Achieving physical goals should not come at the expense of mental health. This chapter explores the importance of striking a balance between pursuing physical excellence and safeguarding mental well-being, promoting a sustainable and holistic approach to personal mastery.

9.   Resilience in the Face of Challenges

Trait Development: Building Mental Toughness

Challenges are inevitable, and mental mastery involves building resilience. Explore the principles of mental toughness, which enable individuals to navigate setbacks, bounce back from adversity, and maintain a positive mindset in the face of life's challenges.

10. The Role of Purpose in Well-Being

Insight: Connecting Physical and Mental Mastery to Purpose

Purpose provides a profound anchor for both physical and mental well-being. This section explores the significance of aligning personal goals with a sense of purpose, fostering motivation, resilience, and a deeper connection to the journey of mastery.

11. Self-Reflection and Mind-Body Awareness

Practice: Cultivating Introspection for Mastery

Achieving mastery involves self-reflection and mind-body awareness. Develop practices that enhance self-awareness, allowing individuals to better understand their physical and mental needs, make informed choices, and navigate the path to holistic well-being.

12. Building a Supportive Environment

Approach: Surrounding Yourself with Positive Influences

The environment plays a crucial role in physical and mental mastery. Explore strategies for creating a supportive environment that nurtures well-being, fosters positive habits, and provides a foundation for sustained growth and fulfillment.

As individuals engage with the principles and strategies outlined in this chapter, they embark on a transformative journey toward physical and mental mastery. By recognizing the interconnectedness of these two dimensions of well-being, individuals can cultivate a lifestyle that not only optimizes physical health and mental resilience but also fosters a harmonious and purpose-driven existence.

5.1 Fitness and Well-being for Alpha Males

The pursuit of fitness and well-being is integral to the lifestyle of the alpha male, combining physical prowess with mental resilience. This section explores the principles and strategies that alpha males embrace to optimize their fitness and overall well-being, aligning these pursuits with their assertive and goal-oriented approach to life.

1.   Physical Strength as a Foundation

Principle: Building Power for Overall Dominance

For the alpha male, physical strength is not just about aesthetics; it forms the foundation for dominance in every aspect of life. This section delves into the importance of strength training, emphasizing the role of functional fitness to enhance overall physical prowess.

2.   Strategic Workout Planning

Approach: Tailoring Fitness Regimens for Alpha Goals

Alpha males approach fitness with strategy. This involves tailoring workout plans to align with specific goals, whether it be muscle building, endurance, or overall athleticism. Strategic planning ensures efficient use of time and resources for maximum impact.

3.   Nutritional Excellence for Peak Performance

Principle: Fueling the Alpha Engine

Nutrition is a key component of alpha male well-being. This section explores the principles of a nutrition plan that supports peak physical and mental performance. From macronutrient balance to strategic supplementation, alpha males prioritize fueling their bodies for optimal function.

4.   Mental Resilience Through Fitness

Insight: Training the Mind alongside the Body

Fitness is not solely a physical endeavor for alpha males; it's a mental discipline. This section explores how workouts contribute to mental resilience, stress management, and the cultivation of a mindset that thrives on challenge and adversity.

5.   Holistic Approach to Well-being

Approach: Integrating Physical and Mental Wellness

Alpha males recognize that well-being is holistic. Beyond physical fitness, mental and emotional health are equally prioritized. This section explores practices such as meditation, mindfulness, and adequate rest as integral components of overall well-being.

6. Discipline and Consistency in Habits

Trait Development: Cultivating Alpha-Mind Discipline

Discipline is a hallmark of alpha males, extending to their fitness and well-being habits. This section delves into the importance of consistency in training, nutrition, and self-care, showcasing how disciplined habits contribute to long-term success.

7. Functional Fitness for Real-World Dominance

Principle: Preparing for Life's Challenges

Functional fitness takes center stage for alpha males, emphasizing exercises that translate to real-world strength and agility. From lifting to functional movements, alpha males train to be physically prepared for the challenges life presents.

8. Balancing Intensity with Recovery

Approach: Optimizing Performance through Rest

Alpha males understand the significance of balancing intense workouts with adequate recovery. This section explores the role of rest, sleep, and active recovery in optimizing physical performance and fostering long-term well-being.

9. Leadership in Group Fitness Dynamics

Approach: Inspiring Through Group Engagement

Alpha males often extend their fitness pursuits to leadership in group dynamics. Whether leading a fitness class, sports team, or workout group, alpha males inspire and motivate others through their commitment and example.

10. Mind-Body Alignment in Goal Achievement

Mindset Shift: Aligning Mental and Physical Objectives

Alpha males adopt a mindset that aligns mental and physical objectives. This section explores how goal-setting, visualization, and a relentless pursuit of excellence contribute to both fitness achievements and broader life success.

11. Adaptability in Training Approaches

Skill Development: Navigating Evolving Fitness Landscapes

Adaptability is a key skill for alpha males in fitness. This section explores how staying informed about evolving training approaches, techniques, and technologies allows alpha males to adapt their fitness strategies for continued growth and results.

12. Mental Toughness in Physical Challenges

Trait Development: Thriving in the Face of Physical Demands

Alpha males cultivate mental toughness through physical challenges. Whether in intense workouts or demanding physical activities, this mental resilience contributes to an alpha mindset that embraces difficulty as an opportunity for growth.

13. Lifestyle Integration for Sustainable Wellness

Approach: Embedding Fitness in Alpha Lifestyle

For alpha males, fitness is not a temporary pursuit but a lifestyle. This section explores how fitness and well-being become integrated into the alpha male's daily life, ensuring sustained health, vitality, and a foundation for continued success.

By embodying these principles and strategies, alpha males optimize their fitness and well-being, creating a powerful synergy between physical prowess and mental resilience. This holistic approach contributes not only to an alpha male's physical dominance but also to a balanced and purposeful life.

5.2 Mental Toughness: The Alpha Mindset

Mental toughness is the bedrock of the alpha mindset, a force that propels individuals beyond challenges, instills resilience, and fuels a relentless pursuit of success. This exploration delves into the core principles and attributes that define mental toughness within the framework of the alpha mindset.

1.   Embracing Challenges as Opportunities

Mindset Shift: Transforming Adversity into Growth

The alpha mindset views challenges not as obstacles but as opportunities for growth. Embracing difficulties with a proactive mindset, alpha individuals understand that each challenge is a chance to refine their mental toughness and emerge stronger on the other side.

2.   Unwavering Self-Belief

Trait: A Rock-Solid Confidence in Abilities

Central to the alpha mindset is an unwavering self-belief. Alpha individuals possess a deep-rooted confidence in their abilities, fostering a mindset that exudes assurance and resilience in the face of uncertainty or setbacks.

3. Resilience in the Face of Setbacks

Trait Development: Bouncing Back Stronger

Mental toughness within the alpha mindset is evidenced by the ability to bounce back from setbacks with resilience. Rather than succumbing to challenges, alpha individuals use setbacks as stepping stones for personal and professional development.

4. Adaptability to Change

Skill: Thriving in Dynamic Environments

The alpha mindset is marked by an innate adaptability. Alpha individuals navigate and thrive in dynamic environments, demonstrating the mental flexibility needed to adjust strategies, overcome unexpected hurdles, and capitalize on opportunities amid change.

5. Focus on Solutions, Not Problems

Approach: Maintaining Solution-Oriented Thinking

Mental toughness in the alpha mindset involves a relentless focus on solutions rather than dwelling on problems. Alpha individuals approach challenges with a strategic mindset, actively seeking and implementing solutions to move forward.

6.   Emotional Control Under Pressure

Skill Development: Mastering Emotional Regulation

Alpha individuals exhibit emotional control even in high-pressure situations. Mental toughness involves mastering emotional regulation, ensuring that decisions and actions are driven by a clear and composed mindset rather than reactive emotions.

7.   Persistence in Pursuit of Goals

Trait: Relentless Pursuit of Excellence

Persistence is a key component of mental toughness within the alpha mindset. Alpha individuals exhibit a relentless pursuit of their goals, persisting in the face of obstacles and setbacks with a determination that propels them forward.

8.   Constructive Self-Talk

Approach: Positive Reinforcement for Success

Mental toughness is reinforced by constructive self-talk. Alpha individuals cultivate a positive inner dialogue that bolsters their confidence, resilience, and overall mental strength, fostering a mindset that propels them toward success.

9. Ownership of Outcomes

Mindset Shift: Taking Full Responsibility

The alpha mindset involves taking ownership of outcomes. Alpha individuals do not shy away from accountability; instead, they embrace full responsibility for their actions and decisions, cultivating a mindset that values accountability and continuous improvement.

10. Learning Orientation

Approach: Extracting Lessons from Experiences

Mental toughness within the alpha mindset is coupled with a learning orientation. Alpha individuals view experiences, both successes and failures, as opportunities for learning and growth, ensuring a continuous evolution toward personal and professional excellence.

11. Time Management and Discipline

Skill Development: Optimizing Productivity through Discipline

Mental toughness requires effective time management and discipline within the alpha mindset. Alpha individuals prioritize tasks, set goals, and maintain a disciplined approach to ensure optimal productivity and progress toward their objectives.

12. Mental Endurance in the Long Game

Trait: Sustaining Focus over the Long Term

The alpha mindset embodies mental endurance for the long game. Alpha individuals exhibit the ability to sustain focus, motivation, and mental toughness over extended periods, allowing them to weather challenges and achieve enduring success.

13. Admiration of Competitors

Mindset Shift: Turning Competition into Inspiration

Rather than viewing competitors as threats, the alpha mindset sees them as sources of inspiration. Alpha individuals acknowledge and respect the strengths of others, leveraging competition to fuel their own continuous improvement and drive for excellence.

In essence, the alpha mindset is a testament to the indomitable spirit of those who embody mental toughness. It's a mindset that thrives on challenges, persists in the face of adversity, and continuously evolves toward greater heights of success. By embracing these principles, individuals can cultivate a mental toughness that not only defines the alpha mindset but also propels them toward unparalleled achievement and fulfillment.

5.3 Stress Management Strategies

In the fast-paced and demanding landscape of modern life, effective stress management is essential for maintaining both physical and mental well-being. By adopting proactive strategies, individuals can navigate challenges, reduce the impact of stressors, and cultivate resilience. This guide outlines practical and holistic stress management strategies for fostering a balanced and thriving life.

1.   Mindfulness Meditation

Practice: Cultivating Present-Moment Awareness

Mindfulness meditation is a powerful tool for stress reduction. By focusing on the present moment without judgment, individuals can alleviate stress and enhance their overall well-being. Regular practice of mindfulness can contribute to increased emotional resilience and a calmer mindset.

2.   Deep Breathing Exercises

Skill Development: Harnessing the Power of Breath

Deep breathing exercises offer a quick and effective way to counteract stress. Techniques such as diaphragmatic breathing or box breathing help activate the body's relaxation response, reducing tension and promoting a sense of calm.

3. Physical Activity and Exercise

Approach: Elevating Mood through Movement

Regular physical activity is a potent stress reducer. Exercise releases endorphins, the body's natural mood lifters, and provides an outlet for accumulated tension. Whether it's a brisk walk, a workout session, or a recreational activity, incorporating movement into daily routines is crucial for stress management.

4. Effective Time Management

Skill Development: Prioritizing and Organizing Tasks

Strategic time management is key to reducing stress. Breaking tasks into manageable segments, setting realistic goals, and prioritizing responsibilities help individuals maintain control over their schedules and minimize the feeling of being overwhelmed.

5. Establishing Healthy Boundaries

Mindset Shift: Safeguarding Personal and Professional Limits

Setting clear boundaries is vital for stress management. Individuals need to define limits on their time, energy, and commitments. Learning to say no when necessary and advocating for personal needs contribute to a healthier work-life balance.

6. Quality Sleep Hygiene

Practice: Prioritizing Rest for Restoration

Adequate and restful sleep is fundamental for stress resilience. Establishing a consistent sleep routine, creating a comfortable sleep environment, and minimizing screen time before bed contribute to better sleep hygiene.

7. Cultivating a Supportive Network

Approach: Seeking and Offering Emotional Support

Social connections play a significant role in stress management. Cultivating a supportive network of friends, family, or colleagues provides a valuable outlet for sharing experiences, gaining perspective, and receiving emotional support during challenging times.

8. Mind-Body Practices (Yoga, Tai Chi)

Practice: Integrating Movement and Mindfulness

Mind-body practices like yoga and Tai Chi combine physical movement with mindfulness, promoting relaxation and stress reduction. These practices enhance flexibility, balance, and mental focus, contributing to an overall sense of well-being.

9. Healthy Nutrition Habits

Approach: Fueling the Body for Resilience

A balanced and nutritious diet is crucial for managing stress. Avoiding excessive caffeine, sugar, and processed foods while incorporating a variety of nutrient-rich foods supports physical health and provides the energy needed to cope with stress.

10. Journaling and Self-Reflection

Practice: Processing Thoughts and Emotions

Journaling offers a constructive outlet for processing thoughts and emotions. Writing down feelings, concerns, and positive experiences can provide clarity, promote self-reflection, and act as a therapeutic tool for stress management.

11. Mindfulness Apps and Resources

Skill Development: Utilizing Guided Meditation and Relaxation Tools

Technology can be harnessed for stress management through mindfulness apps and resources. These tools offer guided meditation sessions, relaxation exercises, and stress-reducing techniques that can be accessed conveniently, fostering a regular practice.

12. Professional Support and Counseling

Approach: Seeking Guidance for Enhanced Coping

When stress becomes overwhelming, seeking professional support is a proactive step. Counselors, therapists, or psychologists can provide valuable strategies for coping with stress, addressing underlying concerns, and building resilience.

13. Hobbies and Leisure Activities

Practice: Engaging in Enjoyable Pursuits

Maintaining hobbies and engaging in leisure activities are essential for stress relief. Whether it's reading, art, music, or outdoor activities, allocating time for enjoyable pursuits contributes to a more balanced and fulfilling lifestyle.

14. Humor and Laughter Therapy

Mindset Shift: Finding Lightness in Challenging Moments

Humor is a natural stress-reliever. Incorporating laughter into daily life, whether through comedy, socializing, or playful activities, can positively impact mood, reduce stress hormones, and foster a more optimistic outlook.

15. *Progressive Muscle Relaxation (PMR)*

Skill Development: Systematic Muscle Tension Release

PMR is a technique involving the progressive tensing and relaxing of muscle groups. This systematic approach helps release physical tension, promotes relaxation, and contributes to an overall sense of calm.

Adopting a combination of these stress management strategies empowers individuals to navigate life's challenges with resilience and maintain a state of overall well-being. By incorporating these practices into daily routines, individuals can proactively manage stress, enhance their coping mechanisms, and foster a healthier and more balanced lifestyle.

Chapter 6: Financial Mastery

In the journey toward financial mastery, one must navigate through the intricate landscape of personal finance, investment strategies, and wealth-building principles. This chapter delves into key concepts and practices that can empower individuals to achieve financial independence and security.

1. Setting Clear Financial Goals

Before embarking on any financial journey, it's crucial to define clear and realistic goals. Whether it's buying a home, saving for education, or retiring comfortably, establishing specific, measurable, achievable, relevant, and time-bound (SMART) goals provides a roadmap for success.

2. Budgeting and Expense Tracking

A cornerstone of financial mastery is effective budgeting. By creating a detailed budget and diligently tracking expenses, individuals gain a comprehensive understanding of their financial inflows and outflows. This awareness enables better decision-making and ensures that money is allocated wisely.

3. Emergency Fund Management

Unforeseen circumstances can disrupt even the most carefully planned financial strategies. Building and maintaining an emergency fund equivalent to three to six months' worth of living expenses provides a financial safety net, allowing individuals to weather unexpected challenges without jeopardizing their long-term goals.

4. Debt Elimination Strategies

Effectively managing and eliminating debt is a pivotal step toward financial mastery. Prioritizing high-interest debts, consolidating loans, and adopting a disciplined repayment plan accelerate the journey to financial freedom.

5. Investment Strategies

Investing is a powerful tool for wealth creation. This section explores various investment vehicles, from traditional stocks and bonds to alternative options like real estate and cryptocurrencies. Understanding risk tolerance, diversification, and market trends is essential for crafting a robust investment strategy.

6. Retirement Planning

Preparing for a comfortable retirement involves strategic planning and consistent contributions to retirement accounts. Whether it's a 401(k), IRA, or other pension plan, individuals must tailor their retirement savings approach to align with their long-term financial objectives.

7. Continuous Learning and Adaptation

The financial landscape is dynamic, and staying informed about market trends, economic shifts, and emerging opportunities is vital. Continuous learning ensures that individuals can adapt their financial strategies to navigate changing circumstances and make informed decisions.

8. Estate Planning

Securing one's legacy involves thoughtful estate planning. This includes creating a will, establishing trusts, and considering tax implications to ensure that assets are distributed according to one's wishes and in the most tax-efficient manner.

9. Mindset and Financial Psychology

Achieving financial mastery requires not only technical knowledge but also a healthy financial mindset. Overcoming limiting beliefs, understanding the psychology of money, and cultivating a positive attitude toward wealth contribute significantly to long-term financial success.

In conclusion, financial mastery is a holistic journey that encompasses goal-setting, disciplined budgeting, strategic investing, and continuous learning. By adopting these principles and practices, individuals can take control of their financial destinies and build a secure and prosperous future.

6.1 Wealth-Building Strategies

Building and accumulating wealth requires a thoughtful and disciplined approach. The following strategies provide a roadmap for individuals seeking to grow their financial assets and achieve long-term prosperity.

1. Save and Invest Regularly

Consistent savings and disciplined investing form the foundation of wealth-building. Setting aside a portion of income each month and investing it wisely allows for the compounding of returns over time. Whether through stocks, bonds, mutual funds, or other investment vehicles, regular contributions contribute significantly to wealth accumulation.

2. Diversify Investments

Diversification is a key risk management strategy. By spreading investments across different asset classes, industries, and geographic regions, individuals can reduce the impact of a poor-performing investment on their overall portfolio. This strategy helps balance risk and potential returns.

3. Take Advantage of Employer-Sponsored Retirement Plans

Participating in employer-sponsored retirement plans, such as 401(k) or similar programs, offers a valuable opportunity for wealth accumulation.

Contributions to these plans are often tax-advantaged, and some employers may even match contributions, providing an additional boost to retirement savings.

4. Real Estate Investment

Real estate can be a powerful wealth-building asset. Whether through property ownership or real estate investment trusts (REITs), real estate provides the potential for appreciation, rental income, and tax advantages. Strategic real estate investments can diversify a portfolio and create long-term wealth.

5. Educate Yourself About Investments

Knowledge is a crucial asset in wealth-building. Understanding the basics of different investment options, market trends, and financial instruments empowers individuals to make informed decisions. Continuous learning about investment strategies and financial markets is key to adapting to changing economic conditions.

6. Entrepreneurship and Business Ownership

Starting a business or owning equity in a successful venture can be a significant wealth-building strategy. Entrepreneurship allows individuals to leverage their skills and passion into financial success. However, it also comes with risks, and careful planning and management are essential for success.

7. Minimize and Manage Debt

Debt can be a significant impediment to wealth-building. Prioritize paying down high-interest debts and avoid accumulating unnecessary liabilities. Managing debt effectively improves financial stability and frees up resources for saving and investing.

8. Create Multiple Streams of Income

Diversifying income streams provides a safety net and accelerates wealth-building. In addition to a primary job, consider alternative sources of income such as side businesses, investments, or passive income streams. Multiple sources of income can enhance financial resilience.

9. Tax-Efficient Strategies

Understanding and implementing tax-efficient strategies can maximize wealth accumulation. This includes taking advantage of tax-advantaged investment accounts, employing tax-loss harvesting, and optimizing the timing of financial transactions to minimize tax liabilities.

10. Long-Term Perspective

Wealth-building is a marathon, not a sprint. Adopting a long-term perspective and staying committed to the chosen strategies, even in the face of short-term market fluctuations, is essential. Patience and discipline are key attributes for successful wealth accumulation.

Incorporating these wealth-building strategies into a comprehensive financial plan can pave the way for long-term financial success and security. Tailoring these strategies to individual circumstances and goals is crucial for creating a personalized path to wealth accumulation.

6.2 Investment Principles for Alpha Males

It's important to note that the term "alpha males" can carry certain stereotypes and may not be inclusive. However, if you're looking for investment principles aimed at individuals who seek assertiveness and confidence in their financial strategies, here are some key principles:

1.   Confidence with Calculated Risks

Alpha males often exude confidence, and in the realm of investments, this confidence should be backed by a thorough understanding of risk. Take calculated risks by researching and analyzing potential investments, understanding the market conditions, and having a clear risk management strategy.

2.   Decisiveness and Swift Action

Alpha males are known for making decisions quickly and decisively. In the world of investments, timing can be crucial. Once you've done your due diligence, be prepared to act swiftly when opportunities arise or to cut losses when necessary.

3.   Continuous Learning and Adaptation

An alpha mindset involves a commitment to continuous improvement. Stay informed about market trends, economic developments, and emerging opportunities. Adapt your investment strategies based on new information and changing circumstances.

4.   Strategic Diversification

While alpha males are often associated with assertiveness, smart investors recognize the importance of strategic diversification. Spread your investments across different asset classes to mitigate risk. Being assertive doesn't mean putting all your eggs in one basket.

5.   Long-Term Vision with Short-Term Agility

Maintain a long-term perspective on your investment goals, but be agile in responding to short-term market fluctuations. An alpha investor understands that market dynamics can change rapidly, and flexibility is key to navigating these changes.

6. Discipline in Financial Planning

Alpha males exhibit discipline in various aspects of their lives, and financial planning is no exception. Establish clear financial goals, adhere to a budget, and consistently save and invest. Discipline forms the foundation for long-term financial success.

7. Network and Collaborate

Forge strong connections within the investment community. Networking provides valuable insights, potential partnerships, and access to diverse perspectives. An alpha investor leverages relationships to stay ahead of market trends and identify new opportunities.

8. Goal-Oriented Investing

Align your investments with specific, measurable, and achievable financial goals. Whether it's retirement, education funding, or wealth preservation, set clear objectives and tailor your investment strategy accordingly.

9. Emotional Resilience

Maintain emotional resilience in the face of market volatility. The ability to stay calm and focused during turbulent times is a hallmark of successful investors. Emotional intelligence is a valuable asset in navigating the ups and downs of financial markets.

10. Transparency and Accountability

Alpha males value transparency and accountability. Apply this principle to your investments by regularly reviewing your portfolio, assessing performance, and holding yourself accountable for the outcomes. Learn from successes and failures alike.

Remember, these principles are not exclusive to any gender or personality type. Successful investing requires a thoughtful, disciplined, and adaptable approach, regardless of individual characteristics. Adjust these principles to suit your personal style and risk tolerance.

6.3 Financial Independence Blueprint

Achieving financial independence is a multifaceted goal that involves careful planning, disciplined execution, and a commitment to long-term success. This blueprint outlines key steps to guide individuals on their journey toward financial independence.

1. Define Your Financial Goals

Clearly articulate your short-term and long-term financial goals. Whether it's buying a home, paying off debt, or retiring early, having well-defined objectives provides a roadmap for your financial journey.

2. Create a Comprehensive Budget

Develop a detailed budget that outlines your income, expenses, and savings goals. Categorize spending, identify areas for potential savings, and allocate funds towards achieving your financial objectives. Regularly review and adjust your budget as circumstances change.

3.   Emergency Fund Establishment

Build a robust emergency fund equivalent to three to six months' worth of living expenses. This financial cushion provides security in case of unexpected expenses or changes in income, allowing you to navigate challenges without jeopardizing your long-term goals.

4.   Debt Elimination Strategy

Prioritize the repayment of high-interest debt. Develop a systematic debt elimination plan, focusing on paying off debts strategically while maintaining a sustainable budget. As debts are paid off, allocate those funds towards savings and investments.

5.   Investment and Wealth Accumulation

Invest wisely to grow your wealth over time. Diversify your investments across different asset classes and maintain a balanced portfolio. Regularly contribute to tax-advantaged accounts such as retirement funds and explore additional investment opportunities aligned with your risk tolerance and financial goals.

6.   Explore Additional Income Streams

Consider alternative sources of income, such as side businesses, freelance work, or passive income streams. Multiple sources of income can accelerate wealth accumulation and provide added financial security.

7.   Retirement Planning

Develop a comprehensive retirement plan that considers your desired retirement lifestyle, estimated expenses, and potential healthcare costs. Regularly review and adjust your retirement savings strategy to ensure it remains aligned with your evolving goals.

8.   Tax Optimization Strategies

Optimize your tax situation by taking advantage of tax-efficient investment accounts, deductions, and credits. Be aware of tax implications when making financial decisions and explore strategies to minimize your tax burden.

9.   Continual Learning and Skill Development

Stay informed about personal finance, investments, and economic trends. Continual learning enhances your financial literacy and empowers you to make informed decisions. Acquire new skills that can potentially increase your earning potential over time.

10. Regular Financial Checkups

Periodically assess your financial progress and adjust your strategies as needed. Regular checkups ensure that you remain on track to achieve your financial independence goals. Be flexible and adapt to changes in your life, the economy, and the financial landscape.

11. Estate Planning

Plan for the distribution of your assets and the protection of your loved ones through estate planning. Create a will, establish trusts if necessary, and ensure that your financial affairs are organized to minimize the burden on your heirs.

12. Mindset and Financial Well-being

Cultivate a positive and disciplined mindset towards money. Understand the emotional aspects of financial decision-making and practice mindfulness to maintain a healthy relationship with your finances.

Remember, achieving financial independence is a gradual process that requires commitment and discipline. Tailor this blueprint to your unique circumstances, and seek professional advice when needed. By following these steps consistently, you can pave the way to a secure and financially independent future.

Conclusion

In the journey through the pages of "Alpha Male: Master the Art of Influence, Dominate Your Domain, and Achieve Success in Every Area of Life," we've explored the essence of what it means to embody strength, confidence, and success in the diverse arenas of life. This guide has sought to distill the principles of the alpha mindset, providing insights and strategies to empower individuals to reach their fullest potential.

Reflecting on the Alpha Mindset

The alpha mindset is not about dominating others; rather, it's about mastering oneself and navigating life with resilience and purpose. Throughout this book, we've emphasized the importance of self-awareness, discipline, and a strategic approach to various aspects of life, from personal relationships to professional endeavors.

Influence and Leadership

A true alpha understands the delicate balance between influence and empathy. Leadership is not about dictating terms but inspiring others to achieve their best. We've explored the art of effective communication, the power of charisma, and the impact of leading by example.

Success Strategies in Every Domain

Success is a multi-faceted jewel, and the alpha male knows how to polish each facet. From career advancement and financial mastery to health and wellness, this book has provided a comprehensive guide to excelling in every area of life. The principles of goal-setting, resilience, and continuous self-improvement have been woven into the fabric of our exploration.

Embracing Challenges and Learning from Setbacks

An alpha male is not immune to challenges; rather, he views them as opportunities for growth. We've discussed the importance of embracing challenges, learning from setbacks, and maintaining a positive mindset even in the face of adversity. True strength lies not in the absence of challenges but in one's ability to overcome them.

A Call to Action

As we conclude this journey, let it be a call to action. Embrace the principles outlined in these pages, not as a rigid set of rules but as a flexible framework for personal development. Whether you identify as an alpha or not, the lessons here are universal and can be applied by anyone seeking self-mastery and success.

The Continuing Journey

Remember that the journey to mastery is ongoing. The alpha male is not a fixed archetype but an evolving individual committed to lifelong learning and growth. Continue to refine your skills, expand your knowledge, and adapt to the ever-changing landscape of life.

Closing Thoughts

In closing, may this book serve as a guide, a source of inspiration, and a catalyst for positive transformation. As you navigate the complexities of life, may you embody the principles of influence, dominate your chosen domains, and achieve success in every facet of your existence.

Go forth with confidence, resilience, and a commitment to becoming the best version of yourself. The path to mastery is yours to forge, and may it be a journey filled with fulfillment, purpose, and the realization of your highest aspirations.

To your success and the mastery of your alpha potential.